TTS PUBLISHING

The Ideas Factory

Activities to inspire creative writing in Years 1 & 2

BOOK 1

Create gripping plots and sensational scenes to hook the reader in

Inspiring writers of all ages to push their creative boundaries

Make writing the first choice activity for all of your pupils

Anna Kaye Forsyth

Title: The Ideas Factory
Book 1: Activities to inspire creative writing
(Years 1–2)

Author: Anna Kaye Forsyth

Designer: Delineate Ltd

Editor: Tanya Tremewan

Book code: PB00057

ISBN: 978-1-908735-37-9

Published: 2012

Publisher: TTS Group Ltd

Park Lane Business Park
Kirkby-in-Ashfield
Notts, NG17 9GU
Tel: 0800 318 686
Fax: 0800 137 525

Website: www.tts-shopping.com

About the author: Anna Kaye Forsyth (BMusEd) is a freelance writer and editor specialising in educational resources and the arts. She has worked in several primary schools, where she developed a love for using creative thinking to stimulate learning. As she is a musician and poet herself, the creative process intrigues her, as does the challenge of helping others to think outside the square.

Contents

Introduction

When presenting a class with a creative writing task, have you ever met with a response such as, "I don't know what to write" or "I can't think of anything"? Like most of us, pupils often need guidance to spark their creative processes and think in new and different ways to generate ideas. This is the point where *The Ideas Factory* series comes in.

This series provides a one-stop-shop of activities and resources for pupils to develop their skills in creative writing and critical thinking. These are skills that will help them to succeed not only at school but in many other areas of their lives.

Book 1 is specifically designed for pupils in Key Stage 1. A useful complement to this resource is *Book 3*, a toolkit packed with resources that will assist you in implementing the activities outlined in this book, as well as in developing a range of activities of your own.

How to use this resource

This resource is both easy to use and versatile. The activities can be done in sequence, as a programme, or individually if you would like to work on a particular area, such as characterisation or plot. *Factory HQ* (at the end of this introduction) is a great place to start: it can point pupils in the right direction whenever they need to find a particular section or kind of activity.

If you are planning an activity of your own and would like an overview of the resources available in this book, see the index on the final page.

Curriculum links

Key Stage 1 (Years 1–2)

Learning strand: 9. Creating and shaping texts
Objectives *Most children learn to:* Write independently and creatively for purpose, pleasure and meaning Make stylistic choices, including vocabulary, literary features and viewpoints or voice
Year 1 Use key features of narrative in their writing Find and use new and interesting words and phrases, including story language
Year 2 Draw on knowledge and experience of texts in deciding and planning what and how to write Sustain form in narrative, including use of person and time

Source: Adapted from the Primary Framework for Literacy and Maths 2006

Key to features

The following features recur throughout this resource.

Turn it on!

These warm-up activities can be used independently or incorporated into every creative writing session to stimulate creativity and get pupils thinking creatively. You could add copies of these activities to a classroom creativity box or pack, which can be used throughout the year.

Line up your tools

Here preparation tasks are identified for the teacher or pupils to complete before the activity begins.

Example: Photocopy the describing cards from the next page.

Find out more

This feature is for pupils who have already grasped the concept and want to take it a step further.

Example: Look up the word *disguise* in a dictionary. Who wears disguises?

Nuts and bolts

This feature explains a term or concept

Example: A **character** is someone in a story. A story usually has several characters.

Factory HQ

Does your story need some characters?

Turn to Section One: Character generator.

Your story needs interesting characters. In this section, we look at how you can write about interesting characters who seem like they are real people.

Do you need help to get the setting right?

Turn to Section Two: Getting the settings.

A setting is the place where your story happens. In this section, we look at how to write about all kinds of settings.

Does the plot make sense?

Turn to Section Three: Plumbing the plot.

The plot is what happens in your story. In this section, we look at how to write about many different things that can happen.

What type of story do you want to write?

Turn to Section Four: Type tap.

You can write all sorts of stories – like adventures, animal stories and funny stories. In this section, we look at how fairy tales work.

Section One: Character generator

Funny faces

Turn it on! Frozen and funny

1. In pairs, take turns to make a funny face and freeze.
2. Describe your partner's funny face to your partner. What do you see?

Making faces

1. In the first row, draw a face in each box to match the word.
2. In the second row, write a word for each face.

Scared	Sad	Angry

My face

I can describe faces.

Nuts and bolts

"I saw his face." What words could we add to this sentence to tell us more about the face? It depends on what we want this character to look like. For example, we could write, "I saw his cheeky, smiling face" or "I saw his grumpy, bumpy face".

Turn it on! The story of a face

Line up your tools

Photocopy the describing faces cards from the following page and cut them out. Have a range of picture books on hand for reference.

1. In pairs, look at a picture book.
2. Choose two faces that look interesting.
3. For each face, choose two describing faces cards that tell you more about it.

Find out more

Choose another body part and write a list of words that tell us more about it.

Face off

1. In the box below, draw or glue a picture of a face.
2. Write down three words to describe the face. You can use words from the describing faces cards, or write some words of your own.

Three words that tell us more about this face:

____

____

____

Describing faces cards

happy	sad	friendly	mean
silly	clever	pretty	scary
young	old	cute	cheeky
scarred	smooth	grubby	clean
hairy	soft		

Hide me!

I can describe different parts of the face.

Turn it on! Tell us more

Fill each gap with one of the words from the box.

yellow	brown	little	huge
long	short	round	pointy

Marty's hair is ______________________________

Tamzin's nose is ______________________________

The monkey's ears are ______________________________

Fran's freckles are ______________________________

All kinds of disguises

Line up your tools

Photocopy Harry the spy and the disguises from the following pages. Cut out the disguises.

1. Match each word with its picture.

beard **scar** **tattoo** **hat** **cap**

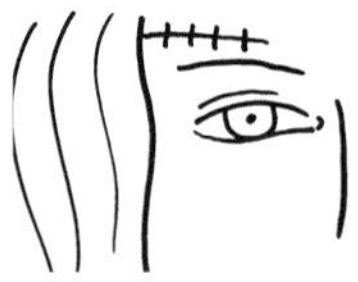

2. Harry is a spy. He has to hide his face. Use the pictures to make two disguises for Harry.

Find out more

Look up the word *disguise* in a dictionary. Who wears disguises?

Harry the spy

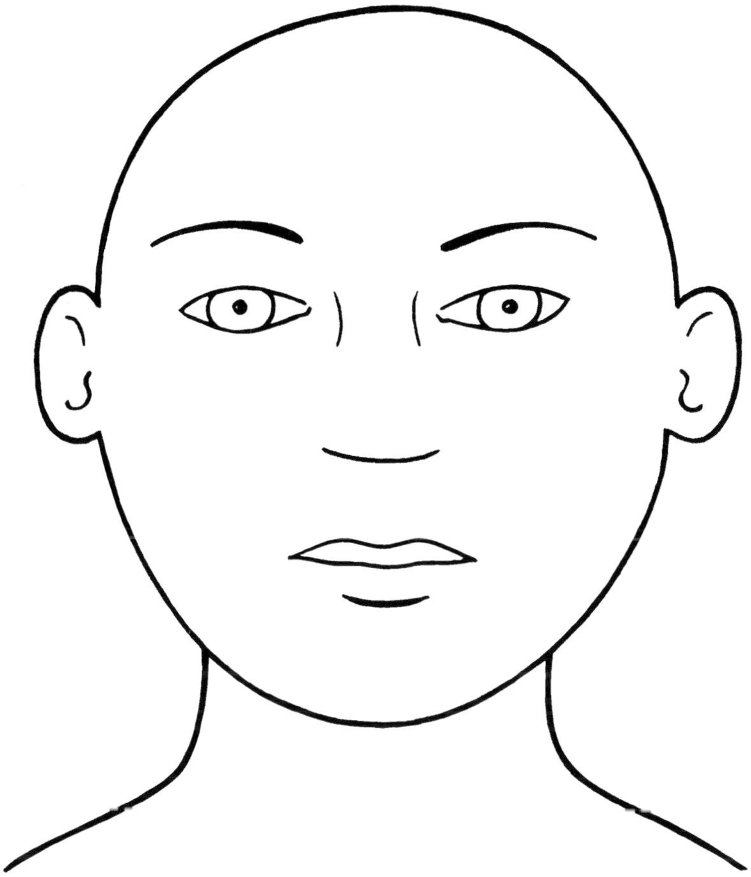

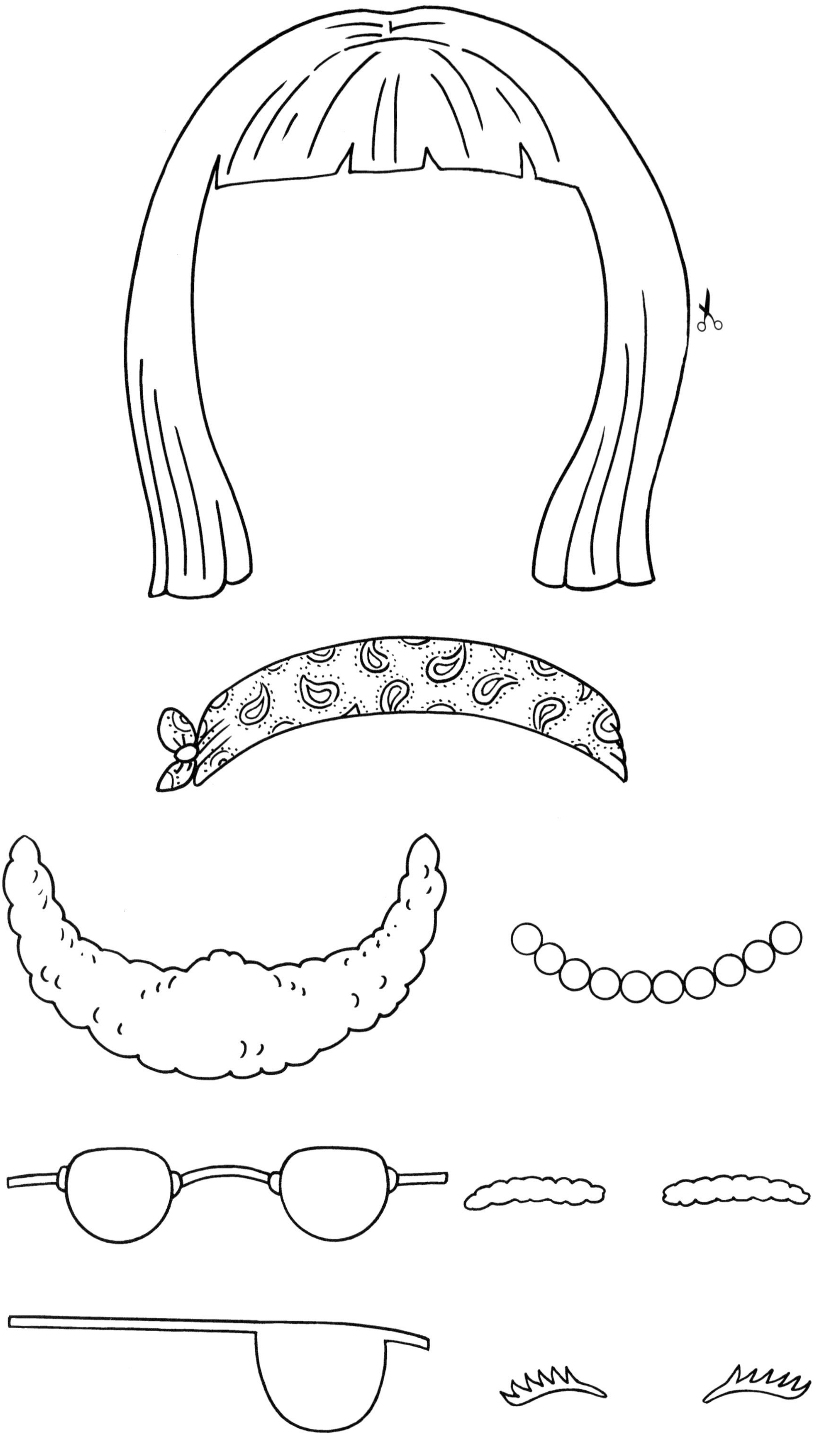

Tell me about them

I can describe a character.

Nuts and bolts

A character is someone in a story. A story usually has several characters.

Turn it on! What kind of worker?

Line up your tools

Photocopy the job cards and describing cards from the following pages and cut them out.

1. In pairs, take turns to pick a job card and a describing card.
2. Join up your two cards and see what they say – for example, *floppy dancer*.

Silly pairs

1. Cut out the words from this page and stick two under each picture on the next page.
2. Draw your own characters in the last two picture boxes. Write words in the blank word boxes to tell more about these characters.

hairy	soft	cuddly	pretty
little	crunchy	sweet	scary
wobbly	good	speedy	shiny
nasty	bad	kind	old
tall	naughty		
young	brave		

			 DL58 AML

police officer	fruit picker	shoe maker	sign writer
shop assistant	mother	vet	singer
builder	clown	nurse	librarian
actor	prison guard	zoo keeper	mechanic

dancer	inventor	teacher	babysitter
cleaner	gardener	cook	athlete
fire fighter	writer	racing car driver	football player
astronaut	farmer	doctor	pilot

fat	blobby	bold	furry
yummy	silly	clumsy	cute
crazy	lazy	floppy	funny
rough	tall	skinny	small

spotty	big	creepy	fierce
slimy	smelly	dirty	ugly
clean	nice	square	gross
lovely	mean	prickly	smooth

Happy families

I can group characteristics together.

Turn it on! You look like ...

Line up your tools

Photocopy the parts of the face cards from the following pages and cut them out.

Make up a funny face. Use the parts of the face cards to get some good ideas about funny features of the face. Do your own drawing of a funny face.

Lots in common

Nuts and bolts

In common means that things, places or people have something about them that is the same.

Line up your tools

Photocopy the "Who am I?" cards from the following pages and cut them out.

You can play this game by yourself or in pairs.

1. Put the "Who am I?" cards in a pile and shuffle them.
2. Pick two cards from the pile.
   - If you think these two people have lots in common (for example, a brother and a sister are two children in the same family), put them in a pair next to you.
   - If you think these two people have nothing in common, keep one card and put the other one back at the bottom of the pile. Then pick a new card from the top of the pile.
3. Continue in this way, trying to make as many pairs as you can of people who have lots in common.
4. Draw "Who am I?" cards for two people that you know on the back of this sheet. Talk with a friend about what these two people have in common.

Parts of the face cards

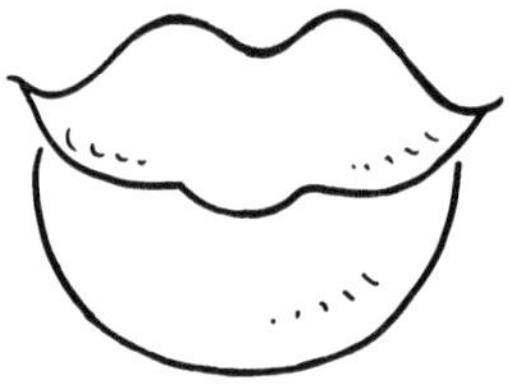

big lips

thin lips

tattoo

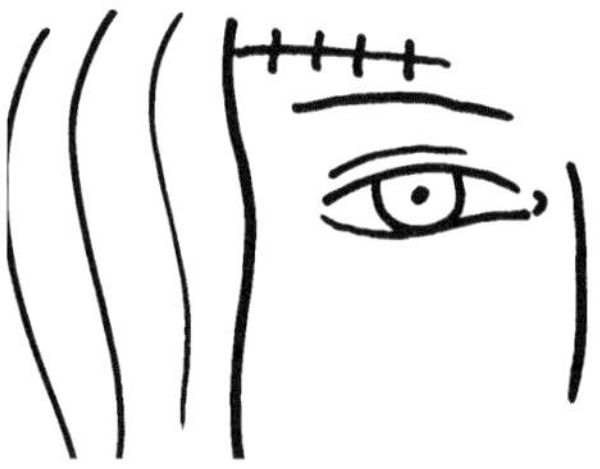

scar

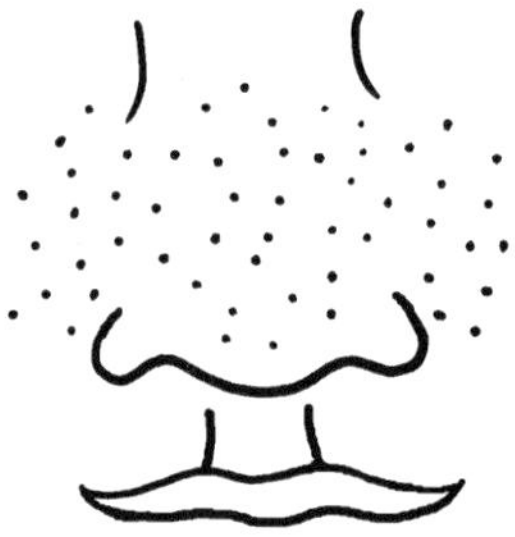

freckles

round eyes

squinting eyes

black eye

thick eyebrows

thin eyebrows

one eyebrow

big nose

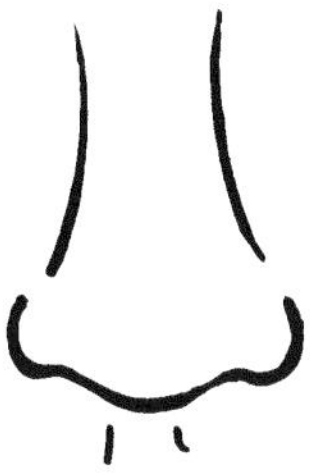

small nose

pointed nose

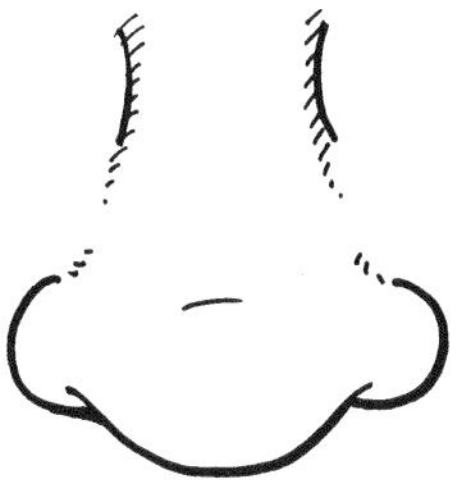

squashed nose

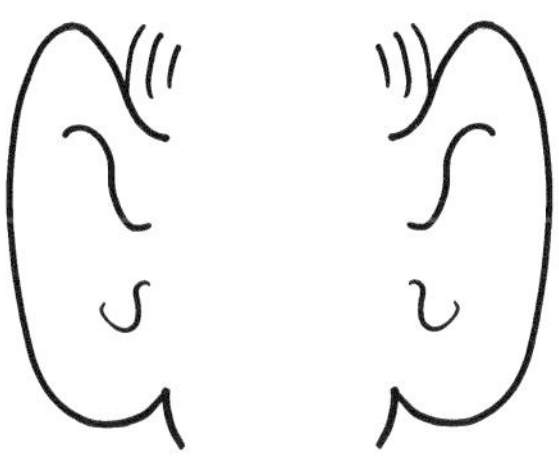

pointy ears

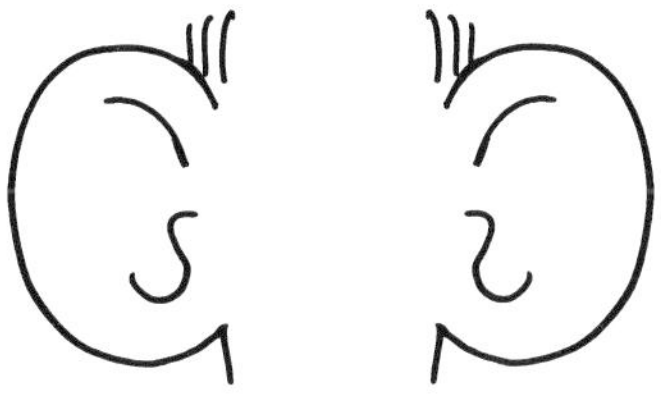

large ears

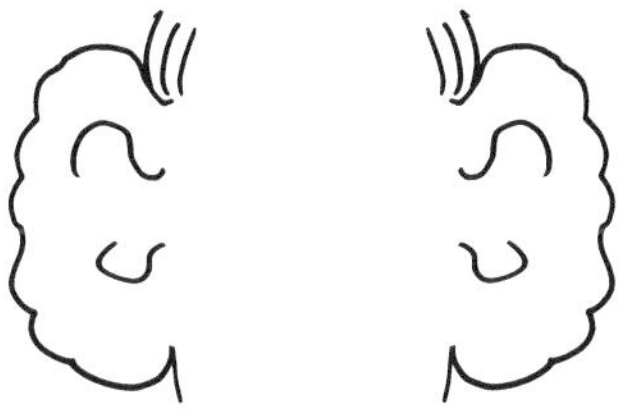

cauliflower ears

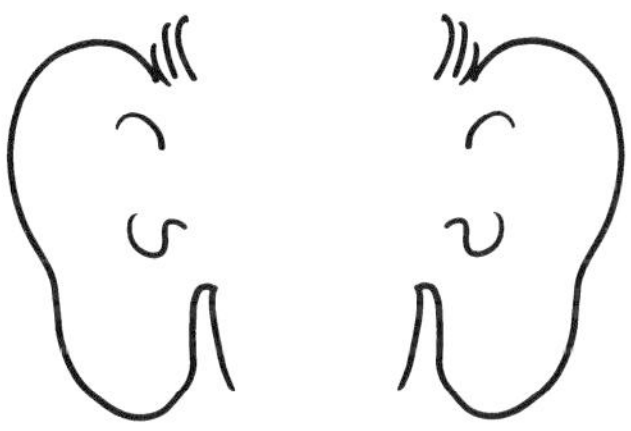

long earlobes

long hair

short hair

curly hair

big eyes

bald

"Who am I?" cards

grandfather	**teenager**	**mother**	**father**
sister	**brother**	**son**	**daughter**
aunty	**uncle**	**grandmother**	**cousin**
wife	**husband**	**helper**	**worker**

grandchild	workmate	team-mate	organiser
oldest	niece	player	boss
youngest	nephew	best friend	boyfriend
baby	servant	neighbour	girlfriend

I spy

I can observe and write from a picture.

Turn it on! Classroom spy

1. Pair up with someone in your class. Take turns to spy on each other for a day.
2. Write down your partner's name and what they do for a day. Write or draw what they look like too.
3. After you have both had a turn at spying, share your findings with your partner.

Keep an eye on them

Look at the picture and answer the questions so that someone who hasn't seen the picture will know what is going on. Choose your answers from the words in the box.

having a picnic	clowns	two
fun, messy people	at the beach	

1. Who are these characters? ______________________
2. How many characters are there? ______________________
3. Where are they? ______________________
4. What are they doing? ______________________
5. What do they look like? ______________________

My friend

I can use pictures to help my writing.

Turn it on! Family facts

Draw a picture of someone in your family. Then fill in the information under the picture.

This person's name is ______________________________

This person is my ______________________________

This person lives in ______________________________

This person likes to eat ______________________________

This person is very good at ______________________________

One thing I like to do with this person is ______________________

____

I decided to draw a picture of this person because ______________

____

Fact file

1. Choose a photo or draw a picture of a friend. Glue it in the box in the middle of the star.
2. Fill in the rest of the star.

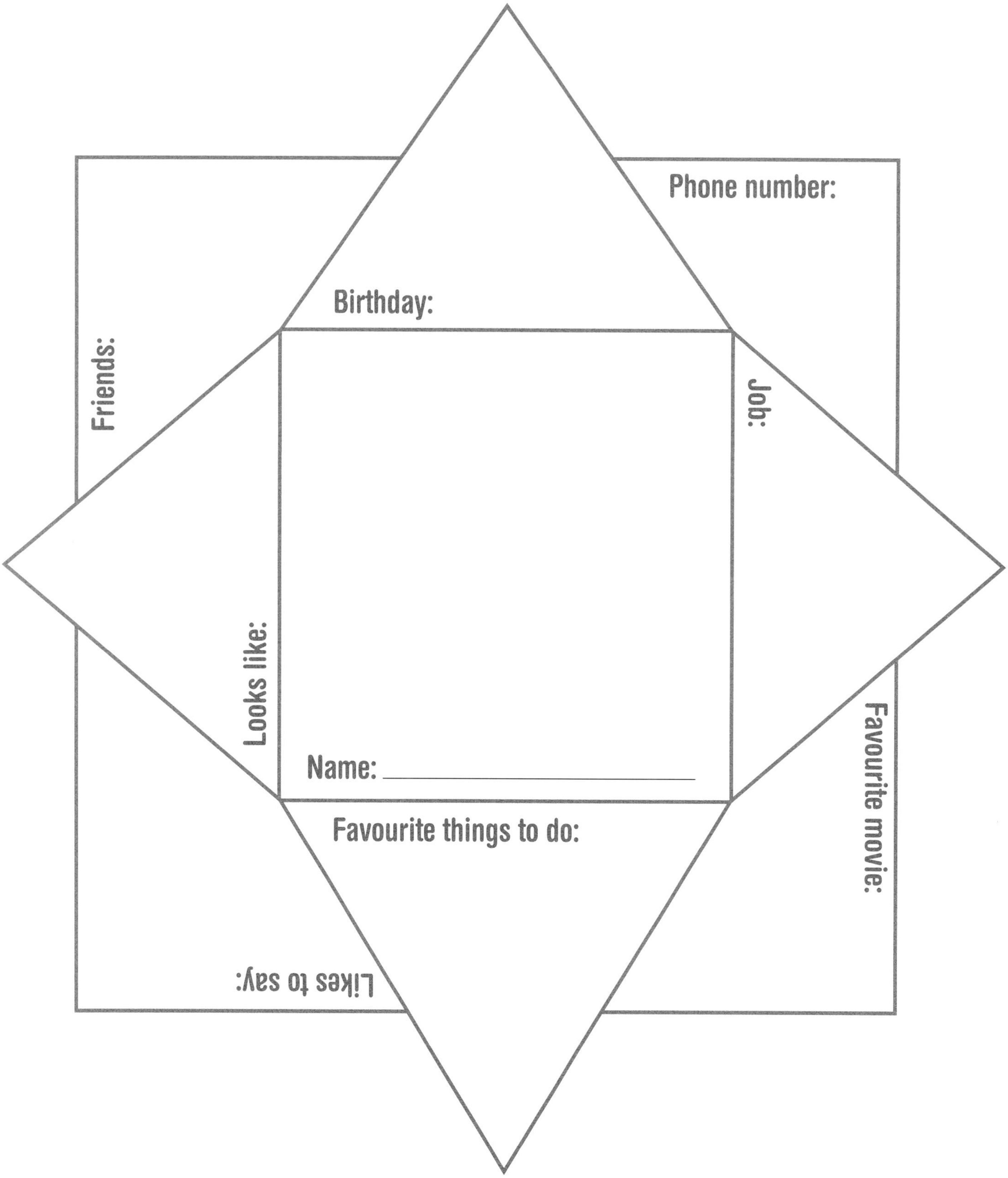

Character generator clipboard

Talk with your teacher about what you found hard and what you learnt in *Section One: Character generator.* Then your teacher can help you to fill in this clipboard.

Funny faces
I learnt

My face
I learnt

Hide me!
I learnt

Tell me about them
I learnt

Happy families
I learnt

I spy
I learnt

My friend
I learnt

Section Two: Getting the settings

At home

I can label the parts of a setting.

Nuts and bolts

A setting is the place where your story happens. For example, it might happen at school, in a hot air balloon or in space.

Turn it on! This is my bedroom

1. Draw a picture of your bedroom.
2. Show your picture to a friend and point out all the different parts of your bedroom.

All about the house

Write a label for each part of this house. Choose the labels from the box.

bathroom	living room	kitchen
laundry	bedroom	

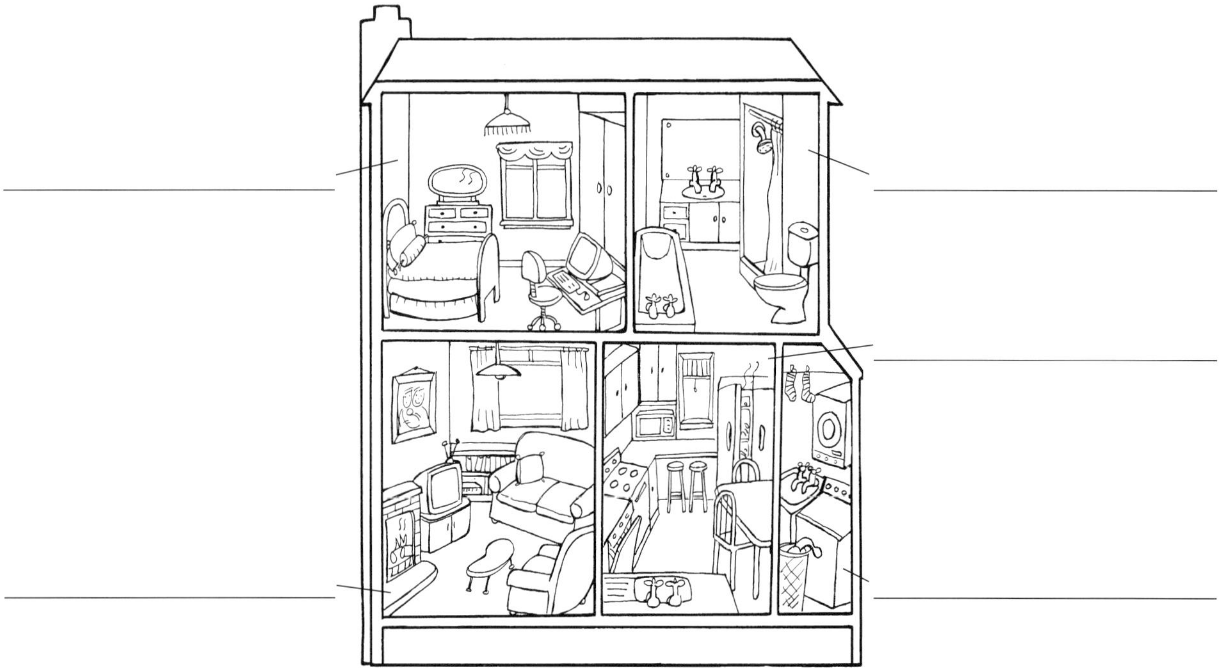

Going places

I can label the parts of a setting.

Turn it on! Go exploring

Make a poster of the jungle **or** the ocean **or** space. Draw five things you might find there.

Where on earth?

1. Cut out the words and stick each one under the right picture.
2. Draw two more settings in the empty picture boxes. Write a label for each one in the blank word boxes and stick them under your drawings.

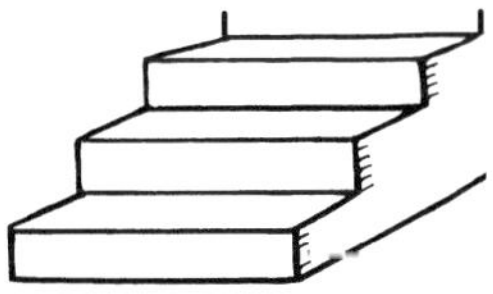	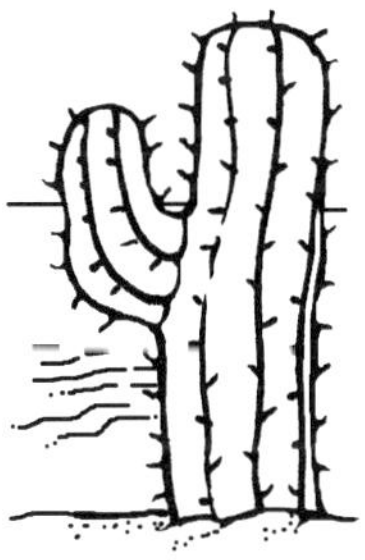		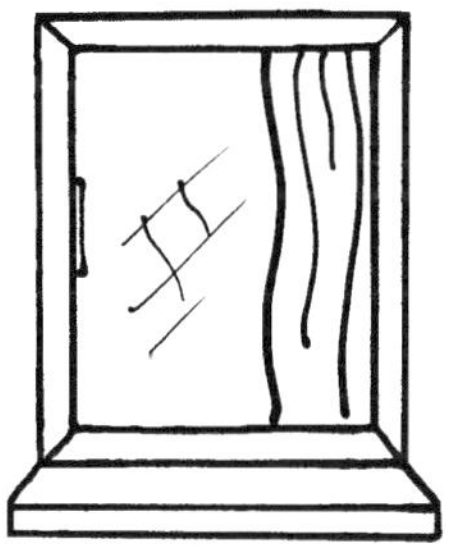

	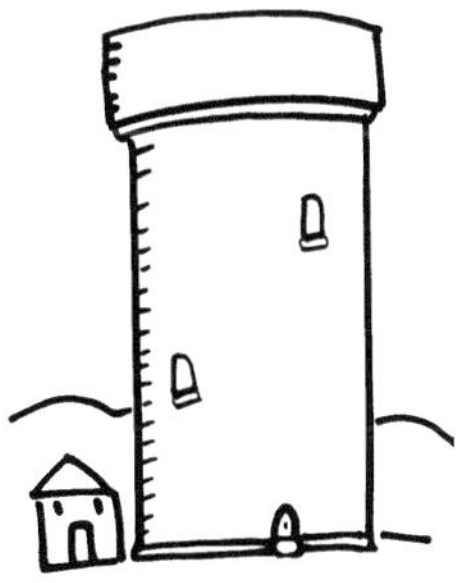		

desert	**window**	**ocean**	
stairs	**tower**	**garden**	

Which setting?

I can label the parts of a setting.

Turn it on! Setting brainstorm

In pairs or as a class, think of all the places or settings that you know.

What did you find there?

1. Cut out the labels. Match each one with the right picture.
2. Copy the label onto another piece of paper. Under it, write some of the things that you can see in the picture it matches.

the forest	**the kitchen**
the circus	**the beach**

Find it!

I can match up different parts to their setting.

Line up your tools

Photocopy the school and circus settings from the following pages.

Turn it on! Room clues

1. In pairs, take turns to think of a room in your house and describe what is in it (eg, "a bed and toys", or "a microwave and plates"). Just give clues – don't tell your partner what the room is called.
2. Your partner tries to guess which room it is. Who can guess with the fewest clues?

School or circus?

1. Cut out the labels. Decide whether each label belongs with the circus or the school.
2. In each setting, do drawings to go with all the labels for that setting.
3. Stick each label next to your drawing for it.

clown	**desks**
acrobat	**dancing dog**
whiteboard	**computer**
paintings	**juggler**
books	**ponies**
teacher	**tightrope**
trapeze	**pencils**

In a circus

In a school

Get set ...

I can create settings.

Line up your tools

Have a range of story books available for reference.

Turn it on! Story setting

Look in a story book that you like. In pairs, talk about these questions.

1. Where is the story happening? (What is its setting?)
2. What things are in this setting to help to show what kind of place it is?

Shoebox setting

Line up your tools

Make several copies of the templates below (as many as needed to create the setting).

1. Choose one of these settings: the zoo, a factory or under the sea. Or choose a different setting from a book that you like.
2. Draw things and people you might see in this setting in the picture boxes.
3. Colour in and decorate your drawings.
4. Cut out your drawings. Glue them onto pieces of cardboard or into a shoebox to make a scene.

Fold this flap	*Fold this flap*

Where's Wanda?

I can guess a scene from clues.

Turn it on! Somewhere you know

1. In pairs, take turns to describe a place you know well. What does it look like, sound like and smell like?
2. Your partner can ask you questions about the place, to find out more about it.

Can you find Wanda?

Write down where Wanda is.

1. Wanda is in ______________________________

I am very cold. I can see lots of ice and penguins.

I am feeling ill. There are lots of beds here. I can see people wearing uniforms.

I am up high. I can see lots of houses under me. Far away I can see grass and trees.

2. Wanda is in

____

____

3. Wanda is in

____

____

I am sitting at a desk. There are children all around me. A grown-up is writing on the whiteboard.

4. Wanda is in ______________________________

Inside or outside?

I can tell the difference between outside and inside words.

Turn it on! In and out

Make a list of inside words and a list of outside words.

Where does this belong?

1. Cut out the cards and stick each one under the correct heading.
2. Think of two more inside words and two more outside words. Write or draw them under the correct heading.

Inside	Outside

pond	**bath**	**boots**	**fish tank**

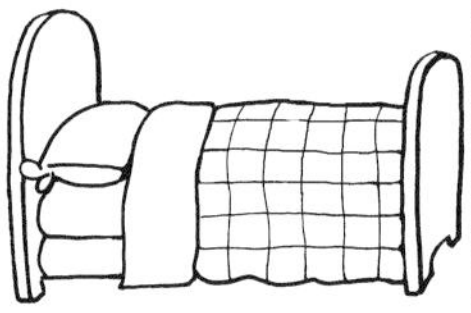

Getting the settings clipboard

Talk with your teacher about what you found hard and what you learnt in *Section Two: Getting the settings*. Then your teacher can help you to fill in this clipboard.

At home
I learnt

Going places
I learnt

Which setting?
I learnt

Find it!
I learnt

Get set …
I learnt

Where's Wanda?
I learnt

Inside or outside
I learnt

Section Three: Plumbing the plot

Cartoons tell a story

I can put events in order.

Turn it on! A funny pair of pictures

1. In pairs, draw two pictures of a funny story you know. One partner draws a picture of the first part of the story, and the other partner draws a picture of the second part of the story. Talk together to decide what you are going to draw before you start.
2. Put the two pictures together when you have both finished.

Order it

1. Cut out each picture and caption below.
2. Put the pictures in order so that they tell a story.
3. Glue the correct caption under each picture.
4. Colour in the pictures.

The police officer tells off Mr Green.

Mr Green takes Fluffy for a walk.

Fluffy is a naughty dog!

What will happen now?

I can talk about what happens before and after.

Turn it on! What if ...?

In pairs, talk about what would happen if ...

- you won a million dollars
- your pet ran away
- you discovered gold
- you broke your leg.

What happens next?

1. Cut out the cards below. Each card tells about an event that happens because of something someone has done before.
2. Stick each card in the right place in the chart on the next page. Each card should show what happens next.

I can't watch any TV for a week!

He slept in my bedroom.

We laughed out loud.

We had to go to a new school.

She couldn't do her homework.

He couldn't go to work.

I had to study harder.

What happened first	What happened next
Mum caught me stealing some sweets.	
My sister broke her arm.	
Dad fell ill and had to go to hospital.	
I forgot some of my spelling words.	
We moved house.	
We saw a funny film.	
My grandad came to stay.	

3. Choose one of the events from the chart above. Talk with a friend about one more thing that could happen **after** "What happened next".

Tell me about it

I can describe what happens.

Turn it on! What happened to you?

In pairs, you both think of something interesting that happened to you in the last week. In turns, ask each other questions to find out as much as you can about this interesting event.

Big questions

1. Think of something funny or exciting that happens in a story (book, film, TV programme) that you enjoy.
2. Now think about what it would be like to be the character in the story during that event. How did you feel? What did you do?
3. Pair up with someone else in your class and ask each other the questions below. Answer as if you are the character in the story you have chosen.
4. Put your partner's answers in the speech bubbles. You can write words or draw a picture to show what they said.

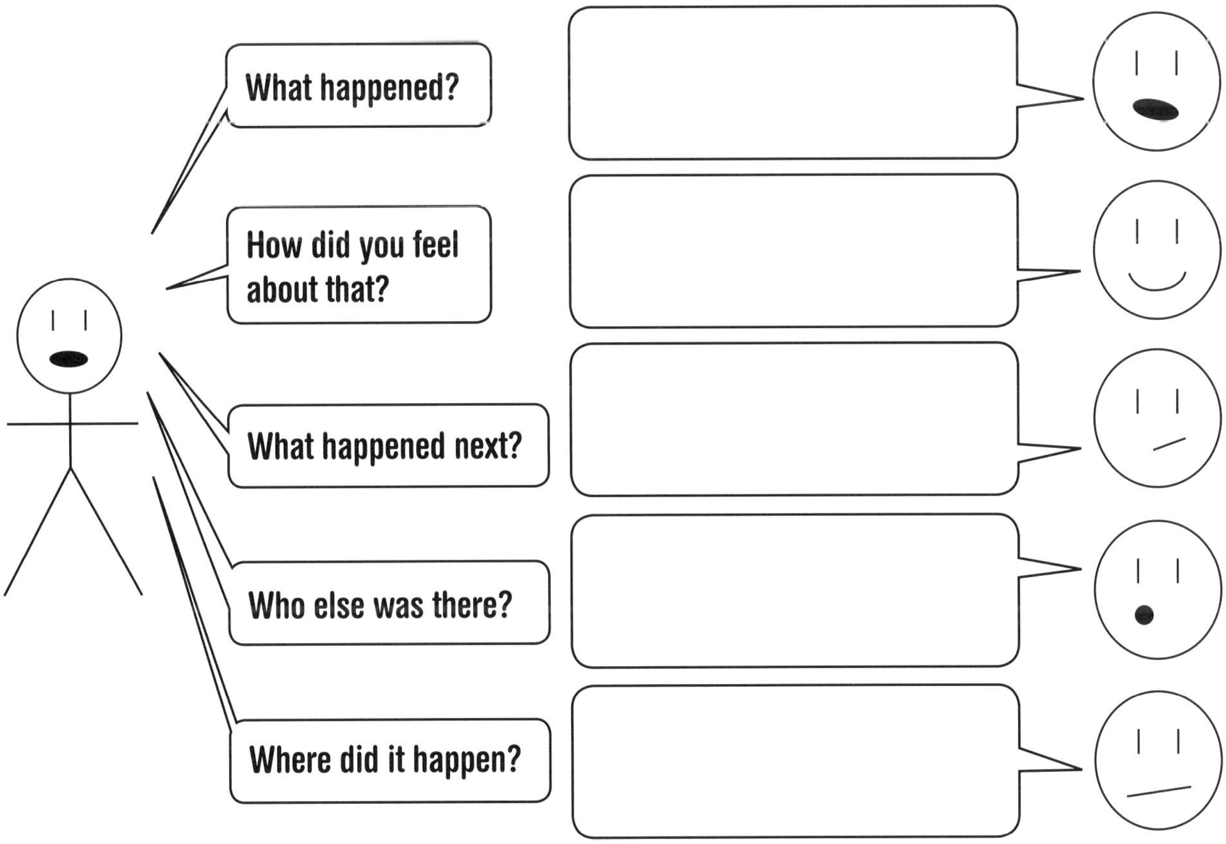

Send me a postcard

I can describe what happens.

Turn it on! Imagine this

In pairs, talk about the kinds of things that might happen if you were:

- an astronaut on the way to Mars
- a film star making a film
- a zoo keeper looking for a runaway lion
- a ghost looking for some people to scare.

What a holiday!

Imagine you have just been on an amazing holiday abroad. Fill in the postcard to a friend telling them about your trip. Use some of the words and ideas in the box if you need some help.

always sunny	snowman	a different way to say "Hello"
skiing	peace and quiet	all day at the beach
yummy food	theme park	thunder and lightning
got lost	cute animals	strange things to eat
stayed up late	big crowds	lots of swimming

Five senses

I can describe what happens through my five senses.

Turn it on! Using all your senses

1. In pairs, talk about what it would be like to be near a big fire. What would you see, hear, touch, taste and smell?
2. In pairs, talk about what it would be like to arrive in Antarctica. Again, what would you notice with each of your five senses?

A big event

What would it feel like to be lost at sea? Think about the words you would use to describe it for all five senses.

1. Write each word from the list below in the right box in the chart.
2. Add another word of your own to each box.

salty lips	giant waves	wet clothes	fishy air
stinging eyes	grey sky	whistling wind	creaking boat

Lost at sea

Sense	Words to describe it
Smell	
Hear	
See	
Taste	
Touch	

Plumbing the plot clipboard

Talk with your teacher about what you found hard and what you learnt in *Section Three: Plumbing the plot*. Then your teacher can help you to fill in this clipboard.

Cartoons tell a story
I learnt

What will happen now?
I learnt

Tell me about it
I learnt

Send me a postcard
I learnt

Five senses
I learnt

Section Four: Type tap - tapping into fairy tales

Fairy tale lines

I can talk about words from fairy tales.

Turn it on! How many do you know?

1. In pairs, think of as many fairy tales as you can.
2. Join up with another pair and see if either pair has thought of any fairy tales that the other pair has not.

The right word for a fairy tale

1. What are the names of these fairy tales? Fill in each blank with one of the words from the box.

Riding	Beauty	New
Pea	Boots	Pigs
Man	Seven	Ugly

(a) Snow White and the ______________________ Dwarfs

(b) The Three Little ________________

(c) Puss in ________________

(d) Little Red ______________________ Hood

(e) The Gingerbread ____________

(f) Sleeping ______________________

(g) The Princess and the ______________________

(h) The Emperor's ______________ Clothes

(i) The ________________ Duckling

2. Here are some words that you often see in fairy tales. Fill in each blank with one of the words from the box.

wicked	land	spell
time	away	prince

(a) Once upon a ____________________ there lived a princess.

(b) The handsome ____________________ came to the rescue.

(c) They lived in a castle far, far ____________________.

(d) She was the most beautiful girl in the ____________________.

(e) The girl had a ____________________ stepmother.

(f) The witch put a ____________________ on the children.

3. Three words at the end of many fairy tales are *happily ever after*. Cut out these pictures and captions, match each picture with its caption, and put them in order so the story ends happily ever after.

The prince came to the rescue.	**The witch cast an evil spell.**	**The prince and princess lived happily ever after.**

The baddies

I can talk about baddies in fairy tales.

Nuts and bolts

The **baddie** in a story does evil things to the main character.

Turn it on! What's so bad about a baddie?

1. Choose **one** of these baddies: Ogre, Big Bad Wolf, Troll.
2. Draw a picture of your baddie that shows why he is bad.

Baddies everywhere

1. Circle the **baddie** in each group.

(a) Red Riding Hood	The Wolf	The Woodcutter
(b) The Witch	Jack	Grandma
(c) Goldilocks	Wicked Stepmother	Little Billy Goat Gruff
(d) The Dragon	The Three Little Pigs	Cinderella

2. Choose a baddie from a fairy tale. Write two evil things that this baddie did.

Name: ____________________

Evil thing 1: ____________________

____

Evil thing 2: ____________________

____

Find out more

Another name for the baddie is the villain. Can you think of any fairy tales where the villain wins? Can you think of any fairy tales that don't have a villain?

The goodies

I can talk about goodies in fairy tales.

Nuts and bolts

A **goodie** is someone in a story who does good things. A goodie can be just a good character, or a character who does something brave or clever to save or help someone else.

Turn it on! Why is a goodie good?

1. Choose **one** of these goodies: Puss in Boots, Snow White, Little Red Hen.
2. Draw a picture of your goodie that shows why they are good.

Goodies everywhere

1. Circle the **goodie** in each group.

(a) Jack	The giant	The cow
(b) Stepmother	Prince Charming	Ugly stepsisters
(c) Sleeping Beauty	Bad fairy	Ogre
(d) Witch	Gretel	Troll

2. What brave or clever thing did these goodies do? Fill each gap with a word from the box.

tricked	killed	ball
slashed	pushed	

(a) The fairy godmother helped Cinderella to get to the ___________.

(b) The prince ___________ through thorns to reach Sleeping Beauty.

(c) Red Riding Hood's Dad ___________ the wolf.

(d) Gretel ___________ the witch into the fire.

(e) Puss in Boots ___________ the ogre into turning into a mouse.

Who is who?

I can talk about goodies and baddies in fairy tales.

Turn it on! Fairy tale friend

1. Choose the fairy tale character who you would most like to be your friend. It might be a goodie (like Cinderella) or a baddie (like the Big Bad Wolf).
2. Draw a picture of the character you have chosen.
3. Show your picture to a friend and tell them three things that you like about this character.

Goodies and baddies

For each of these fairy tales, decide who is the goodie and who is the baddie. Write their name in the correct box in the chart.

Fairy tale	**Characters (goodie or baddie?)**
Snow White and the Seven Dwarves	Prince Charming, stepmother
Jack and the Beanstalk	Giant, Jack
Little Red Riding Hood	Wolf, woodcutter
Three Billy Goats Gruff	Big Billy Goat, troll

Fairy tale	Goodie	Baddie
Snow White		
Jack and the Beanstalk		
Little Red Riding Hood		
Three Billy Goats Gruff		

Far, far away

I can talk about where fairy tales happen.

Turn it on! Where do fairy tales happen?

1. In pairs, talk about the kinds of places where fairy tales happen.
2. Draw one of those places.

Just the place for a fairy tale

1. Circle the place in each group where a fairy tale could happen.

(a) a hotel	a cottage	a café
(b) a playground	a bank	a tower
(c) a supermarket	a farm	a factory

2. Circle the place in each group where a fairy tale could **not** happen.

(a) a castle	a school	a forest
(b) a rocketship	a palace	the countryside
(c) a dungeon	a house	a library

3. Match each of these characters with the right place.

Cinderella

Hansel and Gretel

Big Billy Goat Gruff

First Little Pig

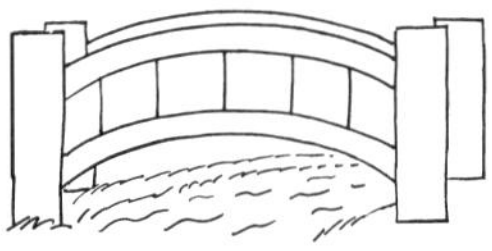

Bits and pieces

I can talk about items that appear in fairy tales.

Line up your tools

Set aside a range of illustrated fairy tales for browsing through.

Turn it on! That's mine

Look at the pictures in a fairy tale.

1. Find the clothes in the story that you would most like to wear.
2. Find a character who is holding or using something that you think looks fun or useful.
3. Draw a picture of yourself wearing the clothes and with the fun or useful thing that you chose.

Who owns it?

What belongs to each of these characters? Match each character with the right picture.

Cinderella

Baby Bear

Little Red Hen

Little Red Riding Hood

Fairy Godmother

Rumplestiltskin

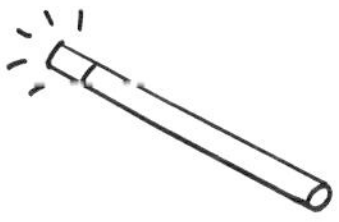

What happens next?

I can talk about what happens in fairy tales.

Turn it on! Do you know this fairy tale?

1. In pairs, each of you chooses a fairy tale (without telling your partner what it is).
2. Tell your partner what happens in the story.
3. Your partner tries to guess the name of the story.

Out of order

Put the events from Cinderella in order.

Cinderella marries Prince Charming.

Cinderella's stepmother makes her clean the fireplace.

The clock strikes 12.

Cinderella loses her slipper.

Prince Charming tries to find the owner of the slipper.

Cinderella goes to the ball.

The fairy godmother gives Cinderella a beautiful dress.

Questions

I can use who, what and where questions.

Line up your tools

Set aside a range of illustrated fairy tales for browsing through.

Turn it on! Questions to talk about

In pairs, choose a fairy tale and talk about these questions.

1. Who are the important characters (main characters) in the story?
2. Who is the **most** important character in the story?
3. What is the story about?
4. Where does the story happen?
5. What happens at the end?

Where are they now?

1. Who is in each of these places? Fill each blank with the name of the right character. Choose the character from the names in the box.

Cinderella	Rapunzel	Jack
The Second Little Pig	Gingerbread Man	Red Riding Hood

(a) ______________________ visits a house in the woods.

(b) ______________________ lives in a house made of sticks.

(c) ______________________ goes to a ball in a palace.

(d) ______________________ runs through the countryside but stops at the river.

(e) ______________________ climbs up a beanstalk to a land in the clouds.

(f) ______________________ lives in a very high tower with only her hair as a ladder.

2. What happens to each character in the place you matched them with in Question 1? Fill each blank with the name of one of the characters in the box.

Cinderella	Rapunzel	Jack
The Second Little Pig	Gingerbread Man	Red Riding Hood

(a) ______________________________ meets a sly fox who says he wants to help.

(b) ______________________________ finds a giant who wants to eat him up.

(c) ______________________________ finds a wolf in her grandmother's bed.

(d) ______________________________ lets down her hair for a prince to climb up.

(e) ______________________________ is frightened when a wolf knocks on his door.

(f) ______________________________ dances every dance with a handsome prince.

3. Where does the baddie find the goodie? Fill each blank with the correct place from the box.

the bridge	the brick house	a cradle
the forest	the seven dwarves' house	

(a) The wicked stepmother finds Snow White in ______________________ ______________________________

(b) The Big Bad Wolf finds the Third Little Pig in ______________________ ______________________________

(c) The troll finds Little Billy Goat Gruff on ______________________

(d) The bad fairy finds baby Sleeping Beauty in ______________________

(e) The Big Bad Wolf finds Red Riding Hood in ______________________

Type tap clipboard

Talk with your teacher about what you found hard and what you learnt in *Section Four: Type tap.* Then your teacher can help you to fill in this clipboard.

Fairy tale lines
I learnt

The baddies
I learnt

The goodies
I learnt

Who is who?
I learnt

Far, far away
I learnt

Bits and pieces
I learnt

What happens next?
I learnt

Questions
I learnt

Index of resources